P57
R135

A DIARY OF PRAYERS
Personal and Public

BOOKS BY JOHN B. COBURN
Published by The Westminster Press

A Diary of Prayers—
Personal and Public

Twentieth-Century Spiritual Letters:
An Introduction to Contemporary Prayer

Prayer and Personal Religion
(Layman's Theological Library)

A Diary
of
Prayers

Personal and Public

by
JOHN B. COBURN

Bowen

THE WESTMINSTER PRESS
Philadelphia

BOOK DESIGN BY DOROTHY ALDEN SMITH

Published by The Westminster Press ®

Philadelphia, Pennsylvania

PRINTED IN THE UNITED STATES OF AMERICA

Library of Congress Cataloging in Publication Data

Coburn, John B
    A diary of prayers, personal and public.

    1. Prayers. I. Title.
BV245.C55   242′.8   75-12824
ISBN 0-664-20823-1
ISBN 0-664-24764-4 pbk.

To all those persons, living and dead, who have been and are special bearers of God to me, beginning with my parents

EUGENIA WOOLFOLK BOWEN COBURN
AARON CUTLER COBURN

O Lord God, who in your Son Jesus Christ have shown us most fully of your love, bless and keep, we pray you, those men, women, and children who also are bearers of your love to us. May we help, not hinder, them in their journey.

Bring us all safe at last to your heavenly home, where we shall live completely in your love and with one another by the strength and in the spirit of him who travels with us, your Son Jesus Christ our Lord.

CONTENTS

II. PUBLIC PRAYERS

Prayers for Worship

*Pastoral Prayers
   and Thanksgivings*

Prayers to Jesus

Prayers for the Social Order

Prayers for the Church Year

PREFACE

There are three strands to this book, sometimes interwoven closely, at other times simply loosely in touch with each other.

For a number of years I have kept what might be called a "diary of prayer." In it I have recorded those experiences which I have tried to work through consciously in relationship to God. They have been pretty much the normal experiences any person goes through. Of some of them I am proud, of others not so proud. What they have in common is my self and my relationship to God. It is the personal I-Thou relationship rising out of my experiences in which I try to relate them to God and to interpret as well as I can what God is doing in and through them. They are human experiences understood (insofar as I can) religiously, that is, by faith.

Therefore, for the most part, the experiences have to do with the people in my life, indeed over the whole of my life. I like most of them, love some of them, have a dislike for a few, and some I just put up with. In every relationship, however, I am aware that God is also involved, that even in those relationships which I find so difficult he is saying something to me, expressing to me some hitherto not clearly understood part of his nature (usually while disclosing some part of mine). In a sense, then, everyone who shares my life is a "God-bearer" to me. To be sure, those who love me and whom I love are more obvious bearers of his love, but even (and sometimes especially) those who do not love me and whom I do not love reveal him to me.

So—as part of my "diary of prayer"—I pray for those who play or have played a significant part in my life, touched me on deep levels, have in part made me who I am. Consciously sometimes, more often unconsciously, they have been bearers of God to me. So I wish to remember them with thanks before God.

These two strands—the human experiences I try to interpret in relationship to God, and the people who make some of the deepest experiences possible—are woven together in the section of prayers called "Personal." They are intensely personal in that they have come out of—been *wrenched* out of—my insides. They are my personal cries to God, and reflections upon what I believe he is doing through the experiences of my life. Obviously, therefore, they reflect my personal relationships. (All revealed here not only resemble persons living or dead but are honest-to-God persons whose only fiction is their names.)

The third strand appears in the section "Public Prayers." These are prayers that have been used on public occasions, written expressly for them. Their connecting link with the other two strands is that, like them, they have been wrung out of my own inner life (*lived,* that is) and are not, therefore, simply "professional" prayers for public occasions. They also arise out of my deep personal convictions about God and his ways with his people.

For whatever purpose these prayers may serve (and they are meant simply to encourage people in their own personal prayers to be as free as they personally can), they reveal as much as I can (not all) of my own personal life in God. Only God knows it all—thank God!

I want to express the deepest appreciation possible to my secretary, who not only deciphered my handwriting, read, criticized, improved, typed, and sometimes censored the manuscript, but who as my wife gave me most of what I have here prayed.

J. B. C.

Duneloch
Wellfleet, Massachusetts

I
PERSONAL PRAYERS

I have been crucified with Christ; it is no longer I who live, but Christ who lives in me; and the life I now live in the flesh I live by faith in the Son of God, who loved me and gave himself for me.

GALATIANS 2:20

Streaking with the Seagulls, Possessed by God

What was I doing, O God, running along the beach at five thirty in the morning, clapping my hands and crying, "O God, I love you, love you, love you"?

Had I taken leave of my senses or come to my senses?

Well, I'll tell you, Lord, what I think—in case it interests you. I think it does, because I think you caused it. *You* possessed me.

If you didn't, then the demons did. And why would demons want me to tell you I loved you?

And why wouldn't you?

So you woke me up at five in the morning. You led me out of bed and down the path over the dunes. You let me hear the birds in the grove in the dawn as I *never* had heard them in my life. You led me to the beach where no person was, no sound but the waves crashing, seagulls crying. You set me off up the beach, over the sand flying (of course not really flying but seeming to fly), the dunes on the left, the breakers on the right. Over the sea the sun's light, first dim, then brighter and brighter. And so far as the eye could see, nothing but nature—sand, water, seagulls—and you.

And when I dove into the waters, it was you I was diving into. When the waters held me up, it was you. When the waves washed me and cleansed me, it was your washing and cleansing. And when I came out, turned, faced the sun and cried, I was crying to you. When I loved the sun and the water, it was you I was loving. When the wind warmed me, it was you.

How could I run so long and not get tired (only that evening did my feet begin to ache)—as though I could run forever? When I clapped my hands, I was applauding you. So I ran and I clapped and I cried, "God, I love you, love you, love you!"

Then I thought of the people I loved, and I put their names in your place—and it was just the same!

"Sam (wherever you are), I love you. Mary, I love you. Pat, I love you. Tom, I love you. Joanna, I love you. God, I love you."

Well, not quite the same, because you are God and they are not. But if it weren't for them, I wouldn't know you, couldn't cry to you, couldn't love you. So I say their names out loud too, though only you can hear me—or maybe through you, in you, they can too. Dear God, I hope so! Pray so!

Makes me realize, such a run as this, I'm not much. That's another reason I think you made me do it. I am just about one of those grains of sand—tossed to and fro, worthless all by myself, never amount to anything if everything left to me.

But in you I am something. In you I am everything. I am part of the sea, belong to it (and even if it's a return to the womb, as some say, or a search for a new womb to enter, if *you* are the womb, then it's a good thing to enter).

I belong to it because I belong to you. And I belong to that sun and to those clouds, and am part of the wind. The clapping that no one can hear but you is not my hands clapping only. It's my heart clapping, my soul. It's *me* clapping. I am applauding the universe, applauding you, me, those I love and love me. So I am somebody because you are you. I am in you. And you in me.

So, you drive me *into* my senses, not out of them. Or, if driven out of them, then only to come *to* them—in you.

"Praise the Lord, my soul. Praise his holy name."

16

How can I not praise you when I know who I am?

That is why I think you possessed me—and I praise you!

But it would have been a little thoughtful of me if I'd left a note for the family saying where I was going at five o'clock in the morning. Sorry, God.

But thanks anyway!

Loose Them and Let Them Go

Easier said than done, Lord. We know it's right —we can't hold on to our children forever. We don't even *want* to. That would be terrible if they never left. Love that holds on destroys. Love that sets free strengthens. So it's right. And we want what is right for them. We loose them and let them go.

But, Lord, the pain! What an ache! Like being torn apart inside.

Still it's right. What if there were no pain? Suppose it didn't make any difference, that we didn't care what they did. Whether they stayed or went.

They *have* to go. It's true to their nature as it's true to ours.

Or I guess it's true to your nature. It has to be somehow—the rightness of pain if life is to go on.

That curious combination, dear Lord, of love and sacrifice, letting go and suffering, pain and joy *together*. It's the keeping of the two together.

And trusting the whole process. We can't manipulate it, can't pick and choose, can't say "I'll take the love" but "No, thanks" to the pain; give me one but not the other.

It's the two together and trusting them together to bring growth and maturity and meaning to everyone who is involved.

That's why there is something of your nature involved: your love. You are love. You express it—in Jesus. *He* expresses it by being obedient to you (love) and inevitably therefore dying, the final separation.

Yet to those who trust, new life comes. Those who believed saw Jesus (or his Spirit) again. So they

18

went on with power and confidence—new, more affirmative people.

So into that love of yours we loose and let go those we love.

Easier said than done. But you help us do it.

Thanks.

How Is It Possible, Lord?

How is it possible, Lord, that I can be caught up entirely with one concern or one cause, or one person, so that is where I "live and move and have my being" and at the same time go about my daily business—answering phone calls, opening mail, attending meetings, eating and sleeping? It's as though I live on two levels—one interior where I *really* live, and the other external where I go through the motions. I am a split personality.

So, how is it possible, Lord, to hold these together without splitting completely?

I don't want to be told to take one or the other, because I just don't believe it's possible—or desirable, for that matter.

That interior part is where I live with richness. It's my loves and thoughts and hopes and prayer. My sins also, and angers and lusts and fears.

The other part is where I go about the business of living in the circumstances of life with the people, responsibilities, and opportunities given me. That is my "vocation"—to live where I have been "called." It's what I get paid a salary for (sometimes overpaid, sometimes underpaid—but not often).

So please don't tell me to exercise my willpower and select one or the other, because that would "split" me indeed. I'd break under the pressure.

I also don't think you can tell me to put those two sides of my nature together so that they become *one*. At least I don't think you can. (But if I knew the answer absolutely, I wouldn't be asking you the question, would I?)

There are so many contradictions, contrarieties, and ambiguities that if I were to try to put the two

20

together so they fit perfectly, then I'd have to chop off so much in both worlds that there wouldn't be much left. I'd have no rages, for instance—and no passion for righteousness, either. Or, rather, the rages would be so controlled, so rational, that all passion would have been squeezed out. You can't make love without passion, can you, Lord? No, I don't think so.

What I am searching for is a way to affirm both parts of life without violating one or the other. How do I keep the furies and the passions harnessed to my reason and my values? I don't see how I can do this, Lord.

—Except in you.

That is, what I really want to do is express *you*—not myself. Or, rather, I want to express myself in and through you and your spirit. You and your spirit hold all things together. Your love fulfills my love and my loves. Therefore as my loves (my life, my goals, my passions, my hopes, and all the rest in *both* sides of my nature) are consistent with your love, then they are fulfilled and I remain in one piece.

I won't therefore have to reject or repress any part of my nature that is consistent with yours. I won't fight my fears or anxieties (or sins, for that matter) but will accept them in order to give them to you so *you* can deal with them as you want to.

I won't reject or repress any loves, either, but will accept them and respond to them in ways appropriate to your nature. Those ways differ from person to person, circumstance to circumstance. So *all* loves are offered to you. You help me respond appropriately—to both your nature and mine.

The point is that I want to affirm life (my own and others') and the only way I can do it is to affirm you. That is (I think) to glorify you.

This is possible, Lord, isn't it?

Holy

Sometimes, O God, I am so bursting with life that all I can say is, "Holy, holy, holy."

Life is glorious because you are glorious.

Or is it that *you* are glorious because life is?

I won't quibble, nor analyze or divide you and life in this way. You are you. Life is life. You are life. And life is you.

You are more than life, dearer than life. Yet since it is only life that brings you to us, only in life are we aware of you, you and life are one—both glorious.

So life is to be glorified—affirmed. As you are.

To be lived, then, affirmatively. Openly. Graciously. How else can we live if we live you—or want to live you?

Not just to live *toward* you but to *live* you.

Not just to say, "Holy, holy, holy" but to *be* holy. Wholly.

Holy Lord. Holy life. Yes.

Holy Ones

If I am bursting with life, I have to burst somewhere, and I want to burst into you.

That is why I say, "Holy, holy, holy"—*you.*

And the only way to burst into you with holiness
is to be holy toward those who bring you—to spill over
with love or affection or whatever is appropriate for the
person at the time. Judgment perhaps.

But whatever it is, what I want it to do is to
glorify you.

Forgive me when I don't.

That is why you are so glorious.

Hi, Holy One!

Hi, all holy ones who bring you!

Holy Cries

It's right at the "bursting point" that I *have* to cry to you. I *have* to say, "Holy, holy, holy" or "Glory be to you, O Lord" or "God" or "Christ" or something. It's right at that point where life seems unbearable that I cry. I say "I'm so happy I could die." Or "Right now I'm ready to die. I am absolutely fulfilled. This is what life is all about."

The "this," dear God, as you know, can be almost anything that seizes, possesses, inspires, exalts. It can be anything from jumping into a snowdrift, turning a somersault into a pile of leaves, diving into a wave, riding a breaker onto a beach, to a kiss, an embrace, a glance—at a person, a mountaintop, the moon—or feeling the wind and so the Spirit moving all the time through everything you have created.

But it's also right at that point where life is so unbearable because it is so awful that I cry. It's when the pain is so terrible, the darkness so black, the waste so meaningless that I cry, "My God."

What the hell is the point of that agony? I just can't stand it. What in Christ's name do you think you are doing? Jesus, I'm going to be split into pieces if you don't hold things together. What drove him to do it? What got into me? How can I bear it?

That's when I cry—when I can't do anything else. Life is so wonderful I can hardly bear it. What goes on, dear God? What are you trying to do?

Are you trying to force these cries out of me? Making it clear I can't make it except in you, in relation to you, maybe even bearing you?

Are these cries of mine maybe yours also? My God, if you who rejoiced at the break of day and grieved at the sorrows of men, who even became sin for us and who broke its power in your Son on the cross when he cried "My God"—boy, if your joy at your creation and your agony at its separation from you were part of my cries of wonder and agony—if you are going through the same things I am going through—then, believe me, Lord, I won't mind crying at all—at least see some point in it—because then somehow my cries glorify you.

And, damn it all, when all is said and done, despite all my selfishness and sensuality and sin, that is what I want to do.

With all my soul I cry unto you.

Holy Kisses

How come, Lord Jesus, that when I blew a kiss at the three nuns who were praying for someone I love they smiled, nodded their heads, and knew exactly what I meant? I loved them, thanked them, told them I was glad they were—all by a blown kiss.

If I hadn't seen them or they hadn't seen me, they would not have known how I felt, would they? The kiss had to be visible, if not tangible.

There is no such thing as a spiritual kiss, is there, Lord? One that is pure spirit, disembodied, no lips touching, no physical contact—a glance if no more?

Well, our spirits keep in touch. But the spirit comes through the body. It has a physical representation. The body bears the spirit, it carries love. And whoever is loved wants to be loved with the body as well as the spirit. Disembodied love becomes vaporous, thin, easily blown away, tenuous.

Or does it, Lord?

Does it have to? Can't my spirit know, be in touch with, penetrate another spirit without the body?

You are spirit, aren't you? Love is spirit, isn't it? And hate and anger and jealousy as well as compassion and caring and agony?

If you are spirit and I know you through the spirit of others, then of course my spirit and theirs can meet out of the body. I can listen to the spirit, can express the spirit, be at one in the spirit, and in fact live in the spirit, by the spirit.

Not completely because the spirit dwells in the flesh, but when the flesh can't touch, the spirit can. The spirit isn't bound by the body, nor by space, not even by time. Why, the spirit can even strengthen the body (as well as weaken it, destroy it).

So when I say, "Our spirits will keep in touch," I mean I will never let *you* go. That is, I won't let you, God, pure spirit, go, because it is only in you I can keep in touch with those whose spirits (and bodies sometimes) I love.

All kisses therefore ought to be holy—that is, carriers of love. Sometimes we kiss with our lips, sometimes we blow our kisses. They always carry our spirit. They are meant to say "I love you, I thank you, I am glad that you are."

That is how I feel about you, Lord, and you're pure spirit, aren't you?

What a Friend We Have in Jesus

I have a friend, Jesus. She is a real *good* friend. She has love, pain, and guts.

When she goes to bed at night, Jesus, she tells me she puts her head on your shoulder and goes off to sleep.

"Jesus, lover of my soul, let me to thy bosom fly."

What a friend I have in her, Jesus.

To be a "friend of the friends of God," Jesus. What friendship you give us in such friends.

Thank you, Jesus, lover of souls.

So now when I pray, let my prayer be,
"Jesus, lover of my soul,
        let me to thy bosom fly
            so I may love
                her, all her friends,
                    all
                You."

Let me learn to love
        Love loving
            You.

It's Devastating, Lord

It's devastating, Lord, but what I most dislike in others is most true of me.

I hate, I despise
      the arrogant and self-righteous.
—So please forgive me my arrogance and self-righteousness.

I hate, I despise
      those men who speak as though they were God.
—So forgive me
      my presumption to act as though I had the inside track on you.

I hate, I despise
      the operators, fawners, look-out-for-number-one-first guys.
—So forgive me
      my cunning opportunism and me-first obsession.

My friend said,
      "You are the most arrogant bastard I have ever known."
Thank you, my friend.
      You are right.
Lord, you thank him.
      You thank the son-of-a-bitch.

It's Not Enough

It's not enough, Lord, to say, *forgive me this, forgive me that, make me a good boy, change that habit, straighten me out.*

Those are the prayers of a lifetime. *Forgive me. Make me a clean heart.* Never again.

God, God—those are stupid prayers. Or inadequate. They don't work. Or they work until I turn around and there I am in the twinkling of an eye right back where I was—maybe worse off, even.

Well, they're not bad prayers. They're not dishonest. They show you I know what I'm like.

But you know that anyway. I'm not giving you information praying like that. It's no news to you, telling you what a bum I am. You know me already.

Take them, please, anyway. Take those stupid prayers. At least they give you some indication I know what I'm like.

But I also know that when I pray like that it's not enough.

What Is Enough?

What is enough is *you.*

I want you. *You* are enough. If I can have you, then what I am like doesn't make much difference.

Or, rather, if I have you, then any difference I make is going to be the difference *you* make.

And you make all the difference in the world—and for eternity, for that matter.

So, when I pray, let me simply wait for you. Let me pray for you. Not anxiously, not beseeching you (though sometimes I have to, I have to knock, plead, bang on the door, demand that you come), but waiting, attending, anticipating, listening, expecting . . .

Expecting *you.* After all, you brought me here. You let me go all over the place, trying all sorts of alternatives to you, turning my back on you, wishing to hell you would go away and leave me alone.

Not only did you bring me here. You turned me to you. You made me pray. More, you *are* the prayer. So, if all I say is "God," it's you praying.

And if you are already praying in me just as I am waiting for you, you are already here. You are already in me.

And that is enough.
That is *everything.*
You.

So, God, here I am waiting.
In you.
Thank you.

31

It's the Damndest Thing

It's the damndest thing, Lord.

Some people have faith because they've worked like hell for it. They have agonized, suffered, held fast, been noble. And, purified, they come into a firm faith.

For others, faith comes as easy as falling off a log. No sweat. They always believed. They never lost hope. Their confidence was never shaken. They always knew you, trusted you, loved you. Easy as pie to have faith for them.

Then the backers and fillers, the on-again, off-again people of faith. Now they have it, now they don't. Now you see it, now you don't. They have it, lost it, find it again. Then it goes away. It dribbles off. They settle for zilch.

Finally, God, all those people who have no faith, never had any, don't want any, say they don't need any, wouldn't know what to do with any if it came their way. It doesn't.

Now, it's the damndest thing, but I've never been able to discern *on the quality of their lives* much of any difference in them.

Some people who have no faith have taught me (and those I love) much about you and how to treat people and how to live with grace, because they were just plain, natural, graceful people.

And some of those who had the deepest faith were the biggest pains in the neck. They blocked you from human sight forever. Any God they believed in they could have. He was no God I wanted.

It's the damndest thing!

Except, I think, for those who suffer. And who suffer in you and with you.

There *does* seem a difference there.
And the difference is that they seem to have a joy
most of the rest of us don't have.
    It's the damndest thing—
        pain emerges as joy,
        sometimes the pain
            doesn't even go away.
        Joy stays with it.
    Damndest thing, Lord.

Finders' Keepers

Dear God,
    e. e. cummings once wrote:
      "whatever we lose—like a you or a me—
      it's always ourselves we find by the sea."
    I say
      Amen.

Why Not, God?

Why not, God, no decision to do anything except glorify you? Why not?

That's a real crisis decision, Lord, one I make when the chips are down, it's all or nothing. I know who I am, what I am here for, where my deepest satisfactions are, what my deepest needs are—and there is no doubt then, no hesitancy, no wishy-washy fussing around.

I know I am here to glorify you, to make you great (if you will pardon the absurdity of it—but the whole process is pretty absurd, when you come to think of it), and then any meaning I am to have is in you. Period.

So in a crisis (like when someone I love dies, or a friend does something awful of which I know I am capable—or even have done and not been found out—or when I am so caught up in love or in compassion that I know exactly what to do, and when who I *am* and what I *do* are exactly the same), I know that I am here to glorify you.

So why not do it?

Well, as you know, I make the decision, and then don't do it—at least not for very long do I do it. Why not, God?

There's got to be some reason. What prevents me? What gets into me? Why do I say next time around when there is no crisis, "Well, I guess I can get away with it once more" or "It can't do any real harm"? God, why the hell does this have to happen? Time after time when I've already told you (time after time) all I want is to glorify you?

Neurosis, perhaps? Perhaps.
Demons, perhaps? Perhaps.
The devil, perhaps?
Perhaps.
In Adam's sin
we all did sin?
Perhaps.
But these don't cut much ice with me, God. They all may be true. But in my guts they don't grip me, so I say, "Aha, that's it. That's why. That explains it." I just don't believe there *is* any explanation (not that it does any harm to fuss around with possible explanations, so long as we don't put any confidence in them).

There isn't any rational explanation that is plausible, reasonable, and convincing. Freud, Marx, and good John Dewey—all thanks to them for the insights they give, but it's deeper, way deeper, the problem lies.

The problem is *you,* dear God. You caused this. You knew what you were about. You created the heavens and the earth, you brought forth all the good things for mankind and raised up the nations and laid down the law and said what's what and "Follow me. And here is my Son, follow him if you can't see me."

So here he is. And here you are. And here am I. And if all I can do is glorify you in him because he is (and therefore you are), then that's what I'll do. Christ, Christ, Christ—*you* do it. That's all I can do.
Thanks. Glory to you.
You do it.
I'm yours.
Thanks.

How Do You Stand It, Lord?

The church, that is.
How do you stand its
    pretense,
        shallowness,
            pettiness,
                meanness, cruelty,
                    corruption,
                        ineffectiveness,
                            junk?
What on earth (or in heaven) do you think when
you look at
            empty liturgies,
                the gospel for comfort only,
                    vying for position,
                        childish, irresponsible actions
                            by prelates, lay popes,
                                clerical bureaucrats,
                                    and pompous clergy
                                        (that's me, Lord),
                    don't rock-the-ship-
                        else-you'll-tip-her-over philosophy?
How come you permit your body—well, that's
what it is—to
            be prostituted by
                me-first,
                    money next,
                        keep-us-going next,
                            outsiders last,

like
blacks,
smelly people,
drunks, drug addicts,
longhairs,
anybody,
anybody different?
Jesus, Lord, how do you stand it?

This Is How I Stand It

    I can't answer for you, Lord. You know I can't. I honestly don't know what you had in mind when you said, "O.K., all my people are going to get together and remember me, and my son Jesus is going to be with them to strengthen them forever." I don't even know if that's what you said, but that's what people said you said, and that's O.K. with me.

    Anyway, this is how I stand it:
        If we didn't have the church,
            where would we go?
        No matter what,
            the church promises something—
that there is more to life than meets the eye,
        that you are,
            that there is hope, meaning, purpose.
            So for Christ's sake don't give up.
And if we walk out, where do we walk to?
        What institutions?
            Schools, colleges,
              Welfare agencies,
              Political parties,
              Labor unions,
                Trade associations,
                  Junior Leagues, DAR's,
                    Country Clubs? What?
What promises *more* than the church?

    So—there is no place else to go. That is a negative reason.
        A positive reason is this:
            People do change, and the reason sometimes is the church.

Sometimes things come together—everything comes together—in the church.

Like life and death
or
Sin and grace.

Hate and reconciliation
or
Pain and joy.

Agony and ecstasy
or
Emptiness and fullness.

Fragments and wholeness
or
Depths and heights.

Yearning and being yearned for
or
Loving and being loved.

Unable to love and being loved forever
or
Being faithless and faithful together.

When everything breaks open, God, is when they
come back together in the church.
It's when a man dies too soon
and grief is sustained by love—
the love of those who love him
and one another
and the love of God in Christ
for him and them
and everybody.

It's when a man and a woman say,
I love you,
and God says,
I do too—forever,
and all who hear
the man and the woman
hear God also.
It's when we know we belong to each other,
when we love (however) everyone (or almost everybody)
and know not only that God loves us and we love God
but that in love we are
in God
and he is in us
forever.
We are *one* in him.
That's the church.
That's how I stand it,
and this
I know
is true.
So I thank you for that
miserable
magnificent
mystery,
your body,
in whom we live
and move
and have our being.

Right Hand, Left Hand

On the right hand, dear God, you gave me reason,
    And on the left, feeling.
On the right, knowledge,
    On the left, intuition.
On the right, decisions,
    On the left, union.
Not one or the other
    But both.

If I think
    and do not feel,
Or reason
    and do not care,
Or act
    without agonizing,
I am nothing.

If I emote
    without thought,
Or intuit
    without ideas,
Or merge into all
    without distinction,
I am nothing.

Together
    the right and the left
        make whole.
Together
    my loves and your truth
        are the same.

Together
    in your love
        I am one with you.

When the right hand knows what the left
    is doing,
And decisions made
    with a whole heart,
Then your holiness
    is affirmed
        by my wholeness.

Don't Waste Pain (I)

"My child, I pray that this pain will not be wasted on you," he wrote her after the death of her daughter.

What did he mean by that, Lord? Don't waste pain! Don't let it slide off into nothingness. Don't drug yourself so the pain is numbed. Then *you* become numbed. What's a numbed person worth?

The pain is so great I can't bear it? Not true. You can bear it. Open yourself to it. *Become* the pain. Then it won't be wasted. Then it will make a difference because *you* will be different.

How not waste pain, Lord?

Well, you don't waste it if you take it, agonize over it, wrestle with it, acknowledge it, see that reason cannot explain it. It's there. Let it come.

Then go about your business. Wake up in the morning and brush your teeth. Go to bed at night with your companion. And in between, go be yourself.

Don't flaunt it. Don't fly it. Don't boast about it. Don't be noble. Don't talk about it except when you must.

Pain is at the heart of the mystery. It is embedded deep in the heart of man and God.

The other side of it is joy.

And with that comes a zest for living.

So live.
> Live your pain,
> > and joy will
> come to live you.
> > Then it's never wasted.

Don't Waste Pain (II)

Let me try this, Lord.
Pain is not wasted
    when
    —it makes clear to us we don't run life,
    when
    —we realize nobody else does either,
    when
    —it ties us more closely
       to our fellow creatures,
          and helps us see
             we all are *creatures*
             and fellows.
Pain proves something, then:
    If
    —it helps us get over
       the passion to think and act
          as though we are *creators.*
          We're not.
    If
    —it chops us down to size
       (very small size, nice and humble).
       If
    —we accept naturally our common creature-
      hood.
If we accept pain,
    we strengthen the fellowship
       of our fellow creatures.
Pain brings power, Lord,
    in some strange way,
       to strengthen life,
          to lift it up,

44

to bring
some nobility to it.
Pain comes as a by-product
when we accept it
as part of our creaturehood,
when we bear it as nobly as we can,
when we offer it to you
because you bore it and said,
"That's how I carry out my Father's
will."
He is the creator, the only one.
We're not.
He redeems his creation, makes it whole again
(or points toward wholeness) by the redeeming power of
his love.

That is how he continues to create.
So we his creatures are part of, participate in, his
re-creating power when, as we accept pain,
we love all the more.
Then pain is *never* wasted.

Why Did He Kill Himself, God?

Or—why did she?

Why does anyone, for that matter?

Or—why doesn't that other person?

Or—why don't I?

God, is there anything worse than having someone I love kill himself? Bang. The end.

Especially when I think—I *know*—there was something I could have done to prevent it. More understanding, more concern, more love, more outreach of hands.

No, I don't *know* that at all. I would like to think I know it, because then I could confess my sin of not loving enough (or intelligently enough), and then I would be forgiven. (You do forgive, don't you, God, if I'm sorry enough?) Then, once forgiven, somehow the suicide is all right. And, even, *I'm* all right.

It won't work, God. It doesn't answer the question, why did he kill himself? Why he and not another whom I have loved even less or worse? It doesn't explain anything. All it does is let me express my feelings, my guilt. God, I want to know about him, not myself.

I just don't know. Probably never will. I know I never will, and if I did know, there is nothing I could do about it anyway.

What I can do is accept it, whatever the reason behind it. I can accept him (or her) as one capable of suicide as I accept myself as one also.

Then I can go on loving a little more than I did before, caring a little more, being a little more sensitive, being more of a person. Perhaps some of his life will come now into my life.

Maybe that's why at least you let him do it, that all who love him may live more fully in his spirit—and yours.

That's what you did when you let your Son die on the cross, wasn't it? So we could all have more life?

So for that sacrifice and my friend's I thank you, and pray that your sacrificial love may dwell more deeply in me.

How Do I Hear You, Lord?

I hear you when
    I accept *everything* about me—
      My sins, my failures and
        the things I don't like
        about myself.
      My gifts, my graces and
        what I've been able to
        do well.
      The circumstances of my life, the people
      around me (just as they are),
        and my past with no regrets.

I hear you when
    I go within
      quietly, honestly, with no
      pretense, no fear.
    Holding up, looking at
      all I see there,
    Not blocking these,
      trying to reject what I see,
        trying to redeem what I see,
          trying to repress what I see,
    Just holding, looking, waiting.

It's then that you come
    as your spirit or something
      I sense, I know, is from you.

Whatever it is,
    it cleanses, accepts, touches
      me—just as I am—
    says you are you,

48

                    don't pretend, don't fake it,
                         don't screw it up.
                            Just be.

Then it (you)
          pulls me gently,
               tugs, teases, calls me
                    to something more,
          says
               "Come on now,
                    there is a lot more,
                         infinitely more.
                         Come on."

And it (you)
          frightens me.
               I have to have what I know,
                    what I control, where I'm boss.
That's scary.
But since it *is* you,
          then it's right.
Which means
          you don't call me to what
          is wrong, morally wrong.
You don't call me
          to sin,
               to selfishness,
                    to unfaithfulness,
                         to irresponsibility,
                         to power.
But to
          rightness,
               wholeness (or more wholeness),
                    excitement,
                         expansiveness (more me),
                              being carried (not

                            49

                                             trying too hard)
Toward *you.*
But you are not so much the goal
            as the way toward the goal.
So I wait for you. Patiently.
            Then you keep me going
                  because I am in you.

In the fullness of time you come, Lord Jesus.
What does it mean, when time is *full?*

It means you, a body in time, bore in that body
eternity—or, perhaps better, eternal love—or, maybe best
of all, God was in you loving us.

So, now in time, when we are loved, we are in
eternity—or, perhaps better, we sense the eternal spirit—
or, maybe best of all, we know we are eternal. When love
comes, *you* come.

It comes. You *come.* We can't create love nor
make you come. We cannot force another to love us—not
our wives or husbands or children or anyone. It's a gift.

All we can do is accept it (you) and respond to it
(you) as we can, now in one way with one person, now in
another way with another, but always accepting, offering,
saying yes to another who comes in time bearing this gift
of eternal life.

So don't let us manipulate time, using the present
to assure the future. Since we cannot create time, only
live in it, let us live in its fullness now. That is to live in
you, in love, when you come, when love comes.

"I Loved Being with You"

When I say to someone, Lord Jesus, "I loved being with you," do I mean, "I love you"?

When I say to you, "I love you, Jesus," do I mean, "I love being with you"?

Of course.

Well, then, when I love someone, you had better see to it that it is *you* loving them—and that they know it—and it is also me.

What Is Your Private Life Like?

When the man asked me, "What is your private life like?" (and turned on his tape recorder) I replied,

"It's walking down through those woods and over those dunes and into that water and sensing God, talking with him, listening to him, being in him.

"It's gathering with my family, being with them, part of them, talking with them, listening to them, belonging to them, being in them.

"It's the people I love and who love me who, when I am with them I am with God and God is with us and in his Spirit we are one.

"It's losing (for the first time) to your son 6–3, 6–3, and the next summer 6–1, 6–1, being annoyed with yourself and with him and proud of him at the same time.

"It's reflecting upon, chewing over, everything, with you.

"O.K., Jesus?"

The Nettle

When the nettle is there, dear God, and it won't
go away,
and I have pretended it would,
hoped it would, prayed it would,
but it won't,

Then help me seize it
gently but firmly
and press.

In seizing it,
may I serve you
without resentment,
without fear,
without regrets.

I want to deal with this nettle
by responding to you
in and with your spirit.

Then if the nettle stays,
I still hold you
gently but firmly,
And on you I *press.*

A Short Prayer in Time of Agony

God!

A Short Prayer in Time of Ecstasy

God!

In the Swirls and Swishes

In the swirls and swishes of life, dear God, we are carried by the currents, ducked by waves, tossed by the torrents, and sometimes float placidly with the tide's ebb and flow.

Amid all these swirls and swishes, give me a temperate spirit, a waiting spirit, a spirit not concerned to get my own way, not vindictive nor boiling with rage.

Keep my deepest instincts anchored in you so where the waves go and I go, I go in you. And we all are carried by the undercurrent of your love into eternity.

In Weakness, Strength

Take my weakness, God.
    Take
        my failures,
        my sins,
        my dishonesties,
            lies, pride, and lusts.

God knows—you know—
    I can't do anything with them.

So, for Christ's sake, take them.

And give me, I pray you,
    not so much a clean spirit,
        nor a pure heart,
        nor a sense of forgiveness—
    give me
        a sense of you,
    of you in me
        and I in you.

Then shall I be strong
    to be
        for you.
    Simply to be.

Anger

Usually, Lord Jesus, when I get angry at somebody, it's because
I'm mad at myself.

I am mad because somewhere
I've let myself down.
So I deal with that by
letting others down.

But when I'm at ease with myself
I'm more at ease with others.
And so they with me.

What I need, therefore, is to keep
ever before me
My true self which
comes only from you
and the depths of my
consciousness.

Keep that image of myself
ever before me
By keeping the image
of yourself
there.

Let us both
drive anger away
(only you can do this for me.
I will cooperate).
Then, being at ease with one another,
I (and you in me)

will love
as I am meant to love.

And don't think I don't get
mad at you, Lord.
I don't want to repress that anger,
I want to express it—
to you
through you
for you
in you.
You then transform it as
you transform me.

Ego Trip

"Some ego trip you were on," my friend commented when I finally finished describing all my recent noble victories.

Boy, was I burned up! Some comment from some friend!

I was so burned up for so long it finally dawned on me he was right.

Dead right.

God!

According to Your Will

Lord Jesus,
    I want to live
        according to your will

And to believe
    it has an eternal meaning.

But to live it anyway.

So I pray:
    O holy one,
        whose holiness
        I become,
        draw me closer
        in your power
        that I may adore
        and live you
        evermore.

Euphoria

There is a euphoria, Lord Jesus, which comes when a decision is carried out that you and I make together.

(I won't argue about who makes the decision or who carries it out,
      You or I.
            It is done, and that's the point.)

So I ask you to keep a gentle reminder before me
      to thank you
           for enabling me
               to join with you—
                   however feebly—
           in carrying out your will
             in living.

Then the euphoria can come and go. It doesn't make any difference.
      You do.

What Do You Want to Do?

What do I want to do for you, Lord Jesus?

Well, I'll tell you.

I want to be faithful to the job
   you have given me to do.

I'd like to lift the vision of the
   people I serve (and my own).

I'd like to make them happy
   in their relationship to you
    (Yes, *happy, blessed*)
   by helping them to deepen
    that relationship.

And to shape myself as well
   as I can
to be a witness to you myself.

That's what I want to do for you, Lord Jesus.

Thank God you said you'd give me
   the power to do it. Thank you for doing it.

Keep After Me

Keep after me, Jesus,
      just the way you have been doing.
Draw me closer
      in the way you have been.

Just keep pressing.
      And help me press back.

Jesus Tiger

You're a tiger, Jesus.
      You just won't let me go.

You sink your teeth in once

And shake and toss and pull

Until I embrace you
      and you embrace me.
            Then I'm yours.

To Be

You are, Jesus.
    I am.

Am in you
    You in me.

No more
    No less.

Just am.

What Did You Do in the Morning of the Night in Which You Were Betrayed?

I'll bet you concentrated on your Father. Period.
Not on all the human agencies which were going
to bring your Father's will to pass, like
                        the government
                            and the soldiers
                                and the high priests
                                    and the crowds.

My guess is that you wanted only to go deeper
into God's mind and will
                    and to rest there trusting him.

Then you let the business of the day begin.

So let us
            morning after morning
    not worry so much about ourselves
                and what's going to happen to us
    but keep our eyes (heart, mind, will)
                on you.

How Do You Treat a Miracle?

There is this sign, Lord, three miles down the barren beach, up against the dunes, and it reads,
This spring is a miracle. Please treat it like one.
And beneath the sign there is a pipe rising out of the dune and a little trickle of water drips through it onto the sand. Nice people must have painted that sign.

So—how do you treat miracles?
Well, gently.
Isn't that how you treat love when it happens? What's more miraculous than somebody loving you?
You must be responsible for that love, Lord, for God knows (you know) I don't deserve love. I'm not what you'd call a lovable person. And yet people love me. And when I say (or they say), "God knows why," that is literally true. Only *you* know.
So let me be gentle with love, with those who love me, and let me thank you for letting them, *making* them love me. You are the maker of miracles.

I don't want to waste miracles nor destroy them. I won't tear up the pipe that bears the water or throw it away. I'll treat it gently. I'll love it, even.

So all who bear your love to me. I'll honor them, reverence them, treat them as holy ones because love is holy, you are holy.
They are holy because they bring me to you.
And I'd like to be holy, too.

Some miracle that would be!

Kept

    If we keep each other in your love, Jesus, then we can say to each other,
        "You're a kept person."
    I like kept people, Jesus. Here are a few more . . .
        You keep them.

A Covenant

    If I have every right to ask you, Jesus, to keep safe from all harm those whom I love,
    You have every right to ask me to live according to your will.
        So as I love them,
            I will.

    With your help.

True Corn

Some corny hymn all right, Jesus:
          "I would be true,
                    for there are those who love me."

True too.
          That's all they want of me,
that I be true
          to you
                    to my self
                              and so to them—

That is love, Jesus.
                    True corn.

Pain + Rightness = Power

"Out of the depths I cry unto you.
      Lord, hear my prayer."

Where else do cries come from but out of the depths? Out
of your guts? Torn from your insides?
      Agony
         Pain
            Crying.

And your answer, Lord, always
      "Be righteous
         "Do right
            "Be somebody
               "Your self."

So Lord,
      I shall live
         by your power
            in your power
               with your power
            in you
               you.

Socrates Said It All—Almost

Socrates said it all, Lord Jesus, when he prayed,
>   *"Beloved Pan, and all ye other gods who haunt
>   this place, give me beauty in the inward soul; and
>   may the outward and the inward man be at one!"*
>   Almost.

What he missed was *you.*

What nature and the gods of nature cannot give,
>   you can.

*So, Lord Jesus (as well as Beloved Pan and all you other
gods),*
>   *"Give me beauty in the inward soul, and may the
>   outward and the inward man be at one!"*

The Difference Between You and Me

The difference between you and me, Jesus, is
    You keep your word.
I don't.

Blessing, Glory, and Honor

"All blessing, glory, and honor be unto you, Lord God of hosts."

You make, break, re-create, encompass, incorporate, fulfill, consummate all agony of my spirit, and all its exaltation. You *have* to hold it all together—all heights, all depths—because I can't.

The agony and the pain, the ecstasy and exaltation, the cries of desolation and songs of joy—all these, I believe, you have put within me. They are yours as much as mine. You are within me, re-creating me, just as much as I am. You and those who brought you within me—all loves, longings, cares, companions, fidelities, and offerings, all aches in my heart, all pains, all hopes.

You brought them, placed them within, became them, moved me within, wrung me, turned me within toward you. Pulled me toward you.

So I hold them all before you now, all agonies, ecstasies, loves, depths and heights, cries and songs. I cannot reject. I cannot repress them. To do so is to reject, repress you.

I offer them to you. I offer myself in them to you. I offer *you* to you in them.

Or—is it you are offering *me?*

Anyway, without you to hold them together, I cannot hold together. In *you* they come together, we came together—now and forever.

So—all blessing, glory, and honor unto you. Lord God of hosts.

Consummation

In you, Lord Jesus,
all things are held together.

All joys and sorrows,
Life and death,
Loves, fulfilled and unfulfilled.

As we trust you with all
these things,
May we go deeper and
deeper into the mystery
of you and your love.
Consummated
in you.
Consumed, to be free.

"Jesus, Whose Name . . ."

Jesus, whose name is above
        every other name
but includes the names of
        all those I love,
I call them by your name
        and call you by theirs.

I cry "Jesus," and the name is "Mary" or "Sam"
        or "Joe," and
I say "Mary" or "Sam" or "Joe," and the name is
        "Jesus."

In you I love them, and in them I love you.

I love you, Jesus,
        Your name above every other name
           As I name those I love . . .

Am I Crazy, God?

I have this deep sense that you are calling me deeper and deeper into you, God, and sometimes I wonder if I'm crazy. If I am crazy and I am in you, then what's so wrong about being crazy?

You say I'm special. I don't say it. *You* say it. Love says it. And I assent to it.

It doesn't mean I'm better. You know that! Or brighter, or holier. It just means that you have had from the beginning of my life (before, even?) a special way with me, a special touch, a special calling for me to be myself in you.

So that when I was most myself I was most in you. I was being what I was meant to be. And who could have been doing the "meaning" but you? So you meant me to be something special in you, in relation to you.

So when I go deeper into you, I go deeper into myself, I become more special. I become more and more myself, I become even a little bit you—what you have in your mind for me. (And have had from eternity?)

But I'm no more special than anybody else. I'm just special in the special way you made me.

Everybody else is just as special—but each in his own special way.

That's not crazy, God. Is it?

If it is, I'm content to be out of my mind and in yours.

It's kind of crazy, isn't it, God?
And I guess that's why you're God
        And we're not.
Crazy.

Alleluia!

76

Clothed in a Spiritual Body

How can I be clothed in a spiritual body, Jesus, when I'm already clothed in a physical body?

You want me to love you with my body, don't you? What's the point of a body if you can't love with it? Isn't that what it's for? How else can I love, amount to anything, mean anything?

So "I" (good old "I"), clothed in a physical body, use it to express my spirit, my love, the "I" which bears your image, love's image, eternity's. My body is love's. (At its best, that is.)

At the moment, since I am not "disembodied spirit," I can love "in the spirit" which is attached to the body. In time (eternity) I shall be (I hope) clothed in a spiritual body. Period. Then we'll let the spirit take care of the spirit.

In the meantime, let me so belong to your spirit that you possess my body, control it, direct it. Let it express *you.* Let love be expressed in ways appropriate to love—not possessing, but accepting, offering, setting free. Let love's body (my body) be the bearer of your spirit to build the spirit of those I love who love me. May our bodies be bearers of that love, not burdens nor destroyers of it. Love builds up, makes the one loved more, not less.

So when hands touch,
may they be warm
with the spirit of your love,
pressing, supporting,
lifting—
never grasping.

You guide them.

77

That our physical bodies now may be clothed in a spiritual body which is yours.

Easier prayed than done, Lord. Right?
Right.

Don't Make Me Good, Lord

Don't make me good, Lord.
    Make me yours.

If all I am is good
    And I give it,
        Then I give myself only.

But if I'm yours
    when I give myself,
        I give you.

And those I love
    don't need me, good or bad.
        They need you.

So, make me yours.

"In the Spirit" (I)

Well, I say to someone, God, "I'll see you in the spirit." Or, "Our spirits will keep in touch." Or, "No, we haven't met before, but I recognize your spirit. I've known it for a long time." Or, "I've known your spirit from before time was."

If I'm going to worship you, God, truly worship you, I worship you "in spirit and in truth." You are pure spirit. How do I worship you truly with my spirit?

When I listen, Lord, *really* listen to others, when they talk (don't talk much myself), then sometimes I hear your spirit. What the words say are not as important as what you say. (In fact, their words may contradict what the spirit says, but the spirit speaks through them anyway.)

And my mind may not clearly understand the words (or may disagree with them, want to argue with them), but I let them go, attentive to the spirit—to their spirit to hear yours.

Then if I can sense this spirit, welcome it, accept it, identify with it, I am "in the spirit." Spirit touches spirit. When those spirits touch, there is *your* spirit.

To rest in the spirit, to help those who speak find their spirit, rest in it (and so in yours), is all I can give them. But that is to give them you. What else is there to give?

Then if they are in touch with their spirit and yours, their words may change. They may come to a better mind. They may make different decisions. That is their business, not mine—or only indirectly mine (a suggestion here, a reflection there).

My business is to affirm them "in the spirit." This is how they are led into *truth*—theirs, which they

80

find in you. To do what is right as you give them to understand the right. So their decisions are made in accordance with their knowledge of your spirit and theirs. That is to set them free—free to be more wholly themselves.

The spirit is deep down. The truth cries out of the depths of the spirit. So we "keep in touch in the spirit."

"In the Spirit" (II)

Now a more personal word, God, about this life
in the spirit in personal relationships. It's not simply that
in our meeting your spirit touches them, but it also
touches me.

And I then deal with your spirit in my own life.
You speak to me through our meeting as much as to
them. You address yourself to my condition as much as
to theirs. So I hear you for myself—so that I may live in
the spirit as well.

If I don't, then there is no spirit of mine made
available to them. I have my own inner, creative growing
edge in the spirit, and as I live along that edge I live in
your spirit and so help bear yours to others. All dialogue
is with you inside.

To live then "in the spirit" negotiating, convers-
ing, attending *you* is what I am about (or meant to be
about).

How shall I describe it?

Heightened awareness?

Expanded consciousness?

An intense concentration of spirit that draws me,
seems to reform me, pulls me more and more out of
myself. To be caught up in your spirit is to be on the
verge of bursting—in (such trite words) love and praise.
It is being transported by your transcendent spirit to be
transformed. That is, you keep wanting to re-create,
transform me more and more into your image, your spirit.
The anguish, the pain, the *joy,* the exaltation—*all together*—are excruciating.

Then, thank God, you bring me back to reality.
When the phone rings, or there is a knock on the door, or

I go buy a hot dog or give somebody a kiss or have to go
to the bathroom.

We can't live by spirit alone. It has to be in *truth*
which is to live in reality as well.

Your Son was *full* of your spirit and truth. So to
enter more deeply into your spirit is to keep an eye on
him—always.

Early-Morning Swim

Why are early-morning swims so refreshing, Lord?

Because the waves wash over me to cleanse me of the sins of the day before?

Sad Certainties

There are certain certainties of life, Lord, that are just plain sad.

There is nothing we can do about them but accept them with as much grace as we can muster.

But if they are certainties, then they came along with you, or you with them.

And you bring all the grace we need—to accept them and, in accepting you, to give thanks for them.

They serve to bring you, so
            for all certainties
                        (seemingly sad),

Thank you.

On Being Patient with God

Time is his,
        Not ours.

In its fullness
        he comes.

Let us wait patiently for him
        and
        for the events
            and people
        that bring him.

Help us to be patient with you,
        waiting
            expectantly.

Lo! He comes, he will surely come.

He has come,
        and his gifts already
            surpass anything
                we might have expected.

So we wait patiently
        for his coming again.
            And again
                and again.

Words for Jesus

Shepherd of the flock
    Lamb of God
        Sacrifice for us

Rock of Ages
    Wisdom
        Eternal Word

Servant
    Son
        Slave

Master
    Teacher
        Lord

Son of Man
    Son of God
        Made sin for us

Man of Sorrows
    Dayspring from on High
        Messiah

Holy
    Lowly
        Glory

On Glorifying God

There are certain times, God, when everything falls together. Family, work, self (inside and outside), friends, people I love, all inner anguish and all inner exaltation—all become one.

They become one in you.

The debris of life—sins, anxieties, failures, guilt —that gets caught up too. That is all overcome, made unimportant—in you, by you. They don't go away. They just fall into place. Trash. Garbage.

Usually after inner stress, or after finishing an assignment, or resolving a conflict, experiencing deep feeling, this sense of completing a chapter, or of fulfilling one's purpose, comes.

The point is, it comes. The fullness of time, the still point. I don't bring it. It comes of its own volition.

Your volition. You bring it. You catch everything up. You pull everything together, give it direction.

I move toward you, in you.
I say, "God" or maybe nothing.
I know then my destiny
to be in you, with you, through you,
with everything and every person
to whom I belong.
Consummation is in you,
on the other side of the grave.
On this side, in the meantime,
Trust
Obedience
Trust
and thanks for everything, everyone.
This is to glorify you.

What Are You Into These Days?

Well, I'm into God.

How else can I get into the people I love? And who love me?

"So 'ham"

That's a mantra, God, in case you were wondering.

"So 'ham." We say it because it means nothing.
    It empties our mind,
        deepens our breathing,
            slows our pulse,
                reduces us to
                    nothing.

Almost.
    But not quite.

Not quite,
    because we left
        the Garden.
    We're out in the great big
        fallen world now.
    We can't go home again,
        can't return to
            animal,
                vegetable,
                    mineral.

No matter how we try.

Now we are spirit,
    now we are self,
        now we are
            more than
            animal,
                vegetable,
                    mineral.

Now we, though still
        bound by nature,
                grounded in it,
are more. We rise
        above it, out of it,
                look at ourselves,
                        look at nature to
                        use it,
                                exploit it,
                                        destroy it
For ourselves.

So the spirit/self
        and the nature/self
        are in a tug-of-war.
                Conflict, choices, decisions,
                        ambiguities,
                                collisions,
                        tensions,
                                dreads,
                                        fears,
                                                anxiousnesses,
                                                clouds.

So no wonder
        "so 'ham"
                appeals.

It does slow down,
        it does bring quiet,
                it does bring peace
                        (sometimes).

"So 'ham"
        strives to empty the self.
                For what?
For the "unified" self.

91

Unity is sought in
            the descent into the one
                  self of nature
                        (vegetable, animal, mineral).
      That is where meaning is found.
            All else is illusion.
      That unity, dear God,
            I seek for as well.

But I find it only in you,
            beyond myself,
                  beyond my self in nature,
                        beyond my self in spirit.

Only in you,
            creator of all nature,
                  including human nature.

And when I
            fell from nature
                  because of my self-
                        will,
I embarked upon all those
            conflicts and conquests,
                  loved and lusted,
                        created and destroyed,
            discovered my life
                  brought with it
                        death.
            So what I wanted to
                  exalt—myself—
                        I guaranteed its
                              ending.
            I am struck down
                  by you.

That is why I turn to
        find my unity
                in you.

I give myself back to you
        from wherever I came
with all my nature,
        animal and spirit,
                loves and hates,
                        rights and wrongs,
                                failures and successes,
                                        fears and joys,
                                                the totality
                                                        of me.

You then do with me what
        you want
                eternally.

In the meantime I will
        say,
                "So 'ham"
        together with,
                "Glory be to you, O God."

What Did the Star Say?

It was quite a while ago, God,
        that we rolled the stone
           over her ashes,
      turned it, shoved it, twisted it
So that the inscription was
      right side up.
           "Into the safekeeping of
               thine eternal love."

Nineteen years ago.

At dusk, in the pine grove,
      on the side of the hill
         (blessed, peaceful spot),
The evening star had
      just come out, and we
         said together, the five of us,
           with one playing in the needles,
         those words,
           and then the prayer
             Jesus taught us.
I trampled the dirt around the stone
      and then looked at the star,
And I wondered,
        What does the star think?
        What can it say?
Nothing
     is what it says.
         Just plain silence.
         No word.
And what does it think?

Only you know.
        All I know is
                it's still there.
As you are.
The star's silence
        is yours.
Its thoughts
        you alone know.
But when you spoke and said,
        "Let there be light,"
You spoke through him who said
        "Our Father . . ."
So through him
        "into the safekeeping
                of thine eternal love . . ."
We commit all whom we love
        and who love us,
                forever.
And the ache never goes away,
        does it?
                Neither do you.
We carry it and you
        into eternity.

What a Difference Death Makes in Making Love

I don't get it, Lord. That is, I don't get it with my mind. Or, rather, my mind only skims the surface, touches, shapes slightly the reality, gives its interpretation, evaluation, description. But it doesn't take hold. It doesn't grab me. The mind doesn't make all that difference.

The difference is down deep—way beneath reason. It's down in the pit of the stomach, it's deep in the heart, it's in your guts, your psyche. It's when you live down deep.

It's where terror strikes. It's when you are frightened, as they say, to death. You are engulfed by wave after wave of anxiety, fear (guilt, perhaps), and you are struck down. Dead. You are no more. Nothing. Washed out to sea. Returned whence you came, nowhere. As though you had never been.

All the aches, pains, loves, accomplishments, angers, exaltations—zip, zero, gone. A little while (a day, a year, a generation, two generations, or three), *nobody* knows you. Wiped out.

That's powerful, Lord. That's dying, death, annihilation. Driven into nothingness.

That's why (I'm not explaining, Lord, I don't understand with my mind. I'm just describing a gut reaction.) the only drive against it, to ward it off, to make believe it isn't there, to overcome it, is the drive to create, to make love. And when you make love in the face of death, you make love differently.

Maybe it's your death. Maybe it's someone else's, someone you love, feel deeply about, hated perhaps, feel guilty about. But when you make love, then death makes you make love differently. More deeply.

It's not just that *you* make love differently. Love makes you make love differently.

The drive to make love drives you to ward off death. If you are possessed by love, then maybe death won't possess you. If you are consumed by love, by the passion of possessing another and being possessed, then you can't, you *can't* ever be nothing. You are something, someone, a body loving another body, a spirit being fulfilled as it fills another spirit. If you die in love's embrace, then the hell with death. If you are spent in love, then death has nothing to embrace.

Love conquers all! Not sexual love alone, though it helps. (Where would we be without it? Not here, anyway. Indeed, we can thank you, God, for it. You made it up. Let us cherish it while we can, embrace it, use it for love.)

That love drive we have for each other to which we belong drives out death for the moment. But the morning comes, and the terror of it rises with us. Another day to reckon with, another day to recognize death, our own and others', to accept it, embrace it.

The embracing of it destroys it. Destroys its power.

Our human love does not do that. Your divine love does. You don't deny death. You rise out of it, born again. That's what love does.

So when we make love, let it be divine love that is made as well as human. Then we shall rise again from the dead.

All of us.

Thanks to you, lovely one. In whom we live, love, die, live again. Forever.

Friends/Enemies

It's a strange thing, Lord, sometimes they switch around. A friend becomes an enemy, an enemy turns out to be a friend.

So I don't draw that line anymore—or try not to.

My enemies sometimes teach me as much about myself (and therefore about you) as my friends do. They help me see my pride, my anger, jealousy, and lack of humility.

They show me my *true* nature. And friends often love me so much they help me hide this side of me from myself (and I try to hide it from you).

So when my enemies come barreling into my life, showing me what I'm like, they make it impossible for me to hide that side from you. You know what I'm like. And now, thanks to them, so do I.

That's a painful truth about me, but since it's the truth, it's revealed by you through them. That is grace—your gift to me, revealing at the same time your nature—
accepting me,
forgiving me,
loving me.

So enemies bring grace, just as friends do. I thank you for them.

And as I cannot reject or repress friends and their love, I'd better not reject or repress enemies and their hate, either. Both I would accept, appropriate, turn into myself, so that

I can return your grace to them,
    turn enemies into friends,
        because both are yours
just as much as I am.

May I be more and more—and they—
    full of grace and truth,
        You.

Arms Stretched at Sunrise

I stretched my arms wide this morning, God. I stretched them wide to encompass the ocean, the sky, the horizon where they meet, the sunrise—and you.

I could not do it.

The reason is obvious. I am not God to encompass his creation.

Why, then, do I want to? What is there in me that wants to take the whole of creation into myself? Why this exuberance? Why this passion to embrace *everything?*

I know I'm not God, and yet I want to be. I'd *love* to love creation, the world, planets, universe, heavens, fog, rain, greatness, and growing things.

I'd love to be God,
and I'm just a hacker like
everybody else.
I'm an earthbound, ashes-to-
ashes, dust-to-dust
creature who will
return right into the
ground. Forever.
So why that embracing?
Why that loving?
Why that holding, caring,
caressing of creation?
Why that consummation
in love?

Have you made me the creature I am—earthbound and loving—so I might see you as you are?

If I—miserable as I am—can love, how much more you can love. If I in such an infantile way can want to embrace creation, maybe this is the only way I can come to see this is your nature—but how much more!

If I in my best moments wouldn't want to harm anybody, then maybe this is how I come to know you love *everybody,* and all creation.

So I'm not going to give up stretching my arms wide to embrace you.

It's the way I know you embrace me,
        everyone,
            everything
                in heaven
                    and earth,
                        forever.

II
PUBLIC PRAYERS

For where two or three are gathered in my name, there am I in the midst of them.

MATTHEW 18:20

PRAYERS FOR WORSHIP

The Worth of Worship

Holy, holy, holy
        Lord God of hosts,
Heaven and earth,
        we, and every living person,
                have some of your glory.
May we all be made full.
Glory be to you, O God most high
        and so low within us.

AMEN

A Prayer for Worship

Lord Jesus, we come now from an unquiet world into your quiet presence. We come with our jumbled, distracted, divided selves to become, if we can, rooted and grounded once again in you. From our frantic, superficial busyness we turn to open ourselves to your peace; from ourselves to you.

We have not been—we confess it now—the persons you want us to be, not even what we want to be. We have not done what we knew perfectly well we ought to have done; and we have done what we knew was wrong and unworthy of us.

We have given way to passions that have lowered us in our own eyes and in the sight of those who know us and love us. We have been silent when we should have spoken, talked when we should have kept quiet. We have walked away from hard issues when we should have seized them as a nettle is seized; and hidden our eyes from things painful and distasteful when we could have brought healing to those who are hurt. When reality has borne in upon us too harshly we have lived by fantasy and run for shelter in the comforts of our dreams. We have built false images of ourselves rather than being true to ourselves.

So, as we seek you in this place, remove first those sins that cloud our sight and dim our vision which we now name before you silently in our hearts . . .

Since you are by faith not only in our hearts but in our midst we also thank you for all the goodness given us, the surprises of grace, the love that has sustained us, the trust placed in us, the encouragement that glimpses of you (visions even) have stirred—even surged—within us.

So these blessings—goodness, people, hope—we also name before you . . . , and we thank you.

Everything that we have been, and everything that we might become meets in you, within us and among us: joys and sorrows, pain and hope, strengths and weaknesses, our light side and our dark side, our worst behind us and our best before us, everything tempered in us and everything eternal. All—and we—meet in you.

We wait now, not so much for a sense of your presence but for yourself—that we may become truly ourselves in you and through you, and then go back into our world to help make it yours, rejoicing, hoping, laughing—with you who have already made it and us your own.

AMEN

Worthy Offerings

You know us, God. You know all about us. We tell you what we want, not to inform you but to be honest with ourselves in your light.

What we want now is to make our offerings to you. Help us to know what to do with those things we want that are not worthy of you or us.

Accept our lives, our loves, our integrity. What we offer to you make whole, so that we may go on from strength to strength and continue to find your meaning in our lives, now and always.

AMEN

God Above Us, Beyond, Around . . .

O God, you are above us, beyond us,
          around us, beneath us, within us.
We sense within ourselves some
          goodness, and we long for more.
We see some beauty around us
          and would bring more to what we see.
We know some truth and search for more
          to be true ourselves.
You are, we believe, the source of all
          that is good and beautiful and true.
So we thank you for what you have already given us.

As we seek more goodness, to create more beauty
          and to know more truth,
Let us remember that you have already found us;
          And that as we live in you, and you in us,
The sense of your presence will grow.
          In that presence goodness, beauty, and truth
               will come as we are able to bear them—
And thus to express them.

AMEN

The Living of Worship

Almighty God, in whose mystery of creating
        and re-creating we have been brought to birth,
Grant us the courage to be ourselves by trusting
          you, so that we may love our
             neighbors as ourselves
and so participate in your eternal process
        of redeeming the world today and always.

A<small>MEN</small>

God of Grace and God of Glory

You are our life and light. You are our journey and our home. In your presence now we ask for nothing save you and your spirit—great, gentle, persistent in your love for us. Glory be to you—God of grace and God of glory.

You are great and greatly to be praised; you are gentle and deeply to be loved. You are persistent in your search for us, and nowhere can we hide from you. So now we face you, ashamed of our weaknesses, thankful for your strength.

A<small>MEN</small>

PASTORAL PRAYERS
AND THANKSGIVINGS

Quest for Identity

Our Father, you made us. You made us so that we are restless until we rest in you. Accept, we beseech you, those pressure points in life where we know we need you. And help us. For you are our Father and we know who we are because you sent your Son, our brother, Jesus Christ.

AMEN

On Becoming Ourselves

Almighty God, help us to become more whole persons. Help us to become more ourselves. As we enter into ourselves, may we come to ourselves so that you may draw us to yourself and to a deeper knowledge of you through our lowliness and service in the name of Jesus Christ our Lord.

AMEN

(Søren Kierkegaard, adapted)

111

Self-Knowledge

Almighty God, give us the gift to see ourselves
       as others see us.
Give us the insight to see within us that self
       which you alone do see.
Give us the courage to be ourselves
       so that we may serve you fully;
Through Jesus Christ our Lord.

A<small>MEN</small>

Self-Respect

O God, help us to respect ourselves as you respect us;
       to accept ourselves as you accept us;
       to forgive ourselves as you forgive us;
       to love ourselves as you love us.
So help us to respect, accept, forgive,
       love our neighbors as ourselves
       in Christ and by the power of his Spirit.

A<small>MEN</small>

Praising and Living

Father, we praise you as we live as you want us to. We know that you will take care of every need we have and that you forgive us as we forgive one another. Help us to remember we are but ordinary men and women—people who need your strength to live wholly as human beings.

AMEN

On Discipleship

Not very good disciples, Lord, but we are disciples. We would like to be. Here we are. Here are our wills, our loves, our conflicts; our irresolutions; our giving way to pressures that are ignobling; our failures to be loyal to love.

Now we hold these before you and offer them to you in your Son in whom we pray—our discipleship in him: "Our Father . . ."

AMEN

Through Weakness, Strength

Let us in God's presence now be absolutely honest with ourselves and with him, and identify those weaknesses

—Where we feel put upon, feeling sorry for ourselves, rather than going about our business in good spirit.

—Being annoyed, short-tempered with others, rather than trying to put ourselves in their place and look at life through their eyes; we must listen to them, try to understand them, accept them, encourage them to be themselves as they believe God wants them to be, not as we believe.

—Being dead certain that I am "the great I am" and that I know what is right all the time with everybody—rather than acknowledge it is usually when two or three are together and agreed that Christ is present, and that most groups are entered into when we say, "I am sorry."

So, God, you take the weaknesses that we have, you take them, they are yours. And by the grace that is in Christ, give us your power so that we may rejoice in our weaknesses to glorify you by having the courage to be ourselves.

AMEN

On Imperfections

Our Father, help us to recognize and acknowledge our imperfections. Here they are . . .

Accept them.

We trust you with them and with us, in your Son, Jesus, our Lord.

AMEN

For the Day

Almighty God, we offer to you now the day which opens before us that we may see you in it as we know you will see us. In everything that comes to us—every grace, every touch of beauty and of life in the world of nature and in human nature—may we sense your presence.

If pain comes, if disappointment or grave distress, may we know that you are present there also to strengthen us and to bless others through us in our enduring without self-pity.

Into your keeping we commit ourselves and all who are dear to us—especially those whom today we shall not see face-to-face but who are, we know, in your presence as we are.

And lest we think only of ourselves, we pray now for those who are lonely, frightened, sick, and those without hope. As you can give them a sense of worth, and the hope that they—as life—must go on.

We want to do what you want done. Help us to accept the demands that life has placed upon us and to accept everybody in it. Help us forgive those we ought to. Let us trust you, and we will trust what happens, on earth and in heaven.

AMEN

A Prayer for Lovers

Lord Jesus,
        great you are in your
                        unrelenting pursuit of us
in the mystery of the love
        given us so we can love.
Help us then to love—as you love—
        without possessing.

AMEN

Love That Holds All Things Together

        Almighty God, we thank you for all those who have been bearers of your grace to us, who have made us more than we are, who have given us the hope of glory, and these we now name before you . . .
        Help us this day to show them our love for them and so your love.
        And now, before you alone, we put ourselves in your hands, trusting you for this life and the life to come, fulfilled in the love that holds all things together—thy Son, Christ our Lord.

AMEN

Friends in Christ

We thank you now for the witness of all who have loved us who now see you face-to-face, our friends in Christ in whom all men are friends and whom we no longer see. We name them . . .

Give them a continuing sense of your presence, grant that we may be bearers of your spirit to our continuing friends—as they are to us.

Bind us in that communion with all prophets who have trusted in you and were not ashamed; so that compassed about with so great a cloud of witnesses we may run with patience the race that is set before us, looking to him who is the author and finisher of our faith, even Jesus Christ our Lord.

AMEN

On Carrying Crosses

Almighty God, we know that you do not deliberately cause us to suffer but that you do enable us to carry our burdens. Grant that we may do so with grace.

There is so much pain in the world, there is so much self-pity in our hearts that we are tempted to forget you because it seems as though you had forgotten us. Keep us from doing this by keeping ever before us the figure of your Son, Jesus Christ, the way he carried his cross, and the power that you brought to the world by his resurrection.

So we offer with him now the pain that is ours, the agony of indecision, the suspicion of betrayal, the fear that we may do wrong because we are wrong, the responsibilities for which we seem inadequate.

We remember that whatever you ask us to do, you help us do it. May we in the light of Christ's victory be strengthened to go on with a lighter step, a renewed sense of purpose, and a vision of the goodness and wholeness that may be ours.

AMEN

Afflictions

Almighty God, accept those areas of our life where we are afflicted.

If it be your will, lift those afflictions.

If not, return them as your gift for the healing of men and for our own hope, joy, and strength; through Christ our Lord.

AMEN

For the Spirit of Christ

Grant to us, O God, more and more of the Spirit of Christ; the Spirit that suffers long and is kind; the Spirit that is magnanimous, generous, noble of purpose; the Spirit that is not stirred to envy, nor moved by self-importance, which does not jealously seek and insist on its rights; the Spirit which pays no attention to the faults of others and tries to believe the best about all men; the Spirit that bears all things, believes all things, endures all things, and which never fails. Through the same Jesus Christ our Lord.

Amen

(William Scarlett, adapted)

A Prayer After Seeing Godspell

O Lord Jesus Christ, who lives within us and among us,
      Lift us to live in accordance with your spirit,
So that we may be risen to live with hope
      And a resurrected life in you,
            raised from the dead,
Abiding with us forever.

                                    AMEN

PRAYERS TO JESUS

The Knock on the Door

You stand, Jesus, at the door of our heart and knock.

We open the door. We invite you in.

As we do so, we thank you not only for the knocking but for the opening.

AMEN

To Will One Thing

Help us, Lord Jesus, Christ, to be at one with ourselves, to be at one with ourselves in you. Refine our confusions, bring order to our disorder. Make us to will in purity of heart one thing only: *you.*

As we are drawn to you, by you, open us to one another. In you may we accept more and more those who are different from us. Make us in purity of heart to will only one thing in them: *you.*

So together may we so live that as we grow into maturity it may be into the measure of the stature of the fullness of your life in us.

AMEN

(Søren Kierkegaard, adapted)

For Trust

Lord Jesus,

We do not understand everything about you, or about ourselves.

But we do know that the more we trust you, the more we know about you and therefore about ourselves.

So we thank you for the little we do understand about you and ask you to help us trust that, so we may grow in knowledge and love of you and of ourselves.

Let us then not worry overmuch about who agrees with us, who disagrees, who is for us, who against us, who understands us, who doesn't care. As we trust you (and life) to do with us as you will, then we shall become more wholly ourselves and members of you.

AMEN

Giving Ourselves and Receiving You

Lord Jesus,

Here are our sorrows and our joys, our fears and our hopes, our failures and our loves.

We name them before you because we cannot resolve, fulfill, complete, make them whole and holy right now.

But we believe you can.

So here they are. You take them. Take us.

And when we receive you in our hearts, give them back to us in you—and therefore in the joy that shall never be taken away.

AMEN

Taking Our Temptations

O Lord Jesus,
>You were faithful to your nature;
>>Help us to be faithful to ours.
>You were obedient to your Father's command
>>to love in your life;
>>Help us obey your commands
>>to love in our life;
>You were tempted and did not sin;
>>We have.

>So we confess our sins to you,
>>and thank you for taking them away.
>When next temptation comes,
>>you take our place,
>>>*you* conquer it.
>>You say no for us,
>>>so we may say yes to ourselves
>And so go on in newness of life
>>praising you for saving us.

AMEN

From Truths to Truth

O Lord Jesus Christ,
    When we are in touch with the truth about
        ourselves,
        we are in touch with you.
    So we thank you for having showed us some
        truth
        about ourselves, and so about you.
    We come to you now because you call us,
        because you have already come to us.
    As we respond to the truths we know,
        so we shall come at last to know you
        who art the Truth.
    In the meantime, help us to live and love you,
        our neighbors, and ourselves.

AMEN

Your Ministry, Your Presence

Jesus,

> You came not to be ministered unto
> but to minister.
> Your ministry was your presence,
> and it still is.
> So we thank you for your presence
> among us and within us.

> Since we are most ourselves
> when we are most attentive to you
> and obey you,
> help us to go about our daily business
> with your spirit
> and to know that when we pray,
> it is you praying within us.

> So may we carry out our ministry
> and yours.

AMEN

On Journey

Lord Jesus,
Leader in our journeys, king of life
and death, and resurrection,
creator of light and darkness,
revealer of mystery and eternity,
don't get too far ahead of us.
But don't let us rest or go back either.

You have called us to life.
Keep us tagging along.
When the crises come, help us
to be true to ourselves, true to you,
and so more ourselves transformed by you
into you so that we may bring life.

And so go on our journey
rejoicing in you and with those
whom you have given us—
our companions along the way.

AMEN

You and Our Loves Together

Lord Jesus,
>You know us better than we
>know ourselves.
>Help us therefore to keep our
>eyes on you, so that we may
>come to ourselves, to be ourselves,
>and so become more you.

>You take our fears now,
>>our anxieties, our worries,
>>and turn them into your own,
>>so that we may be turned away
>>from obsession with ourselves
>>into possession by you.

>We give you also all thoughts
>>that are unworthy of us, all
>>sins that separate us from
>>one another and from you
>>so that we may see more clearly,
>>live more purely, and love more
>>deeply—with our deepest, purest
>>selves.

>Take our longings, our yearnings, and
>>our agonies.
>Transform them as they become yours
>>into joy and glory with peace
>>and love as we become yours.
>We do not want so much the
>>fruits of your spirit as we
>>want *you.*

And we want you for all whom
   we love. So into your care
   we name them as we place them
     that they become themselves in
     you as we in you and you in us
     forever and ever.

AMEN

PRAYERS FOR THE SOCIAL ORDER

Our Father

You—in our heart;
  You—in our nation;
    You—in all men, everywhere;
      You—our Father.

          AMEN

In the beginning was the Truth, and the Truth was with God, and the Truth was God. All things were made by him, and without Truth was not anything made that was made. In the Truth was life, and that life was the light of men. The light of Truth shines in darkness, and the darkness never puts it out. All who bear witness to Truth bring light to all men who come into the world, that they may believe that Truth finally prevails.

So we ask the blessing of God upon the searchers for Truth, and the transmitters of Truth, that they may bring light to the dark places of the world, to the shadowed side of our nation and into the dark recesses of our hearts. May the Truth which alone makes men free strengthen the President of the United States, the Vice-President, and all who have been given the authority of government to execute justice, to maintain peace, to bring hope to all mankind.

And may the same light of Truth illumine the hearts of all the citizens of this land, that honesty, honor, integrity, and compassion may prevail; and that we all may know in our personal lives that the important question is never "Will it work?" but "Is it true?"

So may the moral fiber of this nation be strengthened by us all—in high estate and low—to show forth the glory of God in the life of his people, full of grace and truth.

AMEN

For Systems of Justice

Lord Jesus,
>You were in prison, found guilty when you were
>innocent;
>You were executed as traitor when in fact you
>were Savior.

To you who died to set all men free we pray for:
>All makers of the laws of the land, that they do so
>with reason and compassion.
>All interpreters of the law—judges, lawyers—
>that they be fair, honest, and impartial.
>All administrators of the law—prison guards and
>superintendents—that they be merciful in their
>firmness.
>All prisoners—that they may know that you are
>in prison with them, in their homes with their
>loved ones, and that in you is their hope. Though
>bound, may they be perfectly free in you and in
>your service.

We pray also for the systems that make for peace
in a divided world—journeys of men of goodwill who
meet on neutral ground to bring an end to warfare and
destruction. The cry of anguish of prisoners and innocent
sufferers, of their families, is your cry, Lord Jesus—and
we utter it with you.

So also may the nations united for peace be made
strong. Prosper those who serve the cause of the United
Nations, that together all nations may walk in the ways of
peace and establish an ordered world of justice and
decency for all men.

Finally, Lord Jesus, since you are the light of the world, we pray that you will light up our lives when we are in darkness, that we may live as children of light in peace and love with one another and with you.

AMEN

For Prisoners

When we visit those who are in prison, Lord, we visit you. We go when messengers go on our behalf—chaplains, doctors, social workers, probation officers, ordinary lay people who simply "visit." We pray that as they go from us they may bear the spirit of Jesus to the prisoners who wait for them and that they make him visible.

We pray now, Lord, for
—those who are in prison, for whatever reason
—those who put them there
—victims of their crime
—police, prosecutors, judges
—those who guard them.

We pray for
—their families at home,
that they may not forget them
—those who led them to crime,
that they may come to a better mind
—their companions,
that they may learn
from their experience.

We pray also that all who surround them—guards, teachers, doctors, social workers, administrators, probation officers—may not become hardened in their hearts, calloused, insensitive, bored, but may know themselves as fellow human beings, not faultless themselves, so that
they may serve faithfully
with compassion and

concern
in good spirit and
(when possible)
good humor.

We pray for
—the society which shares some measure of
guilt for its structures of injustice, bigotry, and oppres-
sion which spawns conditions that make for crime
—employers who may provide honest wages
for honest work upon their return
—all people and organizations which work
for reconciliation and redemption.

Finally, we pray for
ourselves,
fellow sinners,
whose hope, as
theirs, is in
the same Jesus Christ
in prison,
in our society,
in our homes,
and in our hearts.

AMEN

For the Nations

From the Koran
In the Name of God, the Merciful, the Compas-
sionate!
Praise be to God, who the three worlds made.
The Merciful, the Compassionate.
The King of the Day of Fate.
Thee alone do we worship, and of Thee alone do
we ask aid.
Guide us to the path that is straight.
The path of those to whom Thy love is great,
  Not those in whom is hate,
  Nor they that deviate.

God *is one God; the eternal God:*
he begetteth not, neither is he begotten
and there is not any one like unto him.

Merciful God, one God in your holy Word, among
your signs are "the creation of the heavens and of the
earth; and the variety of your languages and of your
complexions: verily herein are signs unto men of understanding."
  Therefore we pray for understanding among the
peoples of your world in their variety of tongues, in their
differences of color, in their various national loyalties,
and in their differing witnesses to you.
  We pray that justice and freedom among the
nations may establish the order which reflects your unity.
We pray that the strong may have compassion toward the
weak; that the rich may be generous to the poor; and that

139

those secure in their homelands may sustain the homeless in their journey homeward. May the brothers and sisters of mankind help one another because you are the father of all of us.

You have said, O God, in your holy Word, "I have prepared for my righteous servants what eye hath not seen, nor hath ear heard, nor hath entered into the heart of men to conceive."

So, bless, we pray you, all your righteous servants who are the leaders of their nations, their people, and their families. Give them understanding to know your righteous will, and conform their will to yours. Since you have prepared for them more than the heart of men can conceive, we commend them to you, confident that you will give them both the power and the grace to do that which you have called them to do.

> *Bismillah!*
> *La ilaha illa 'Llah*
> *Muhammadun' rasulu 'Llah.*

AMEN

For Statesmanship

O God of hope, who have made of one blood all nations of men for to dwell upon the face of the whole earth, and who have given your spirit to dwell in the hearts of all men: grant that we may be drawn together by that hope which springs eternally from the deepest longings of mankind, you who have placed that hope within us, help us to live in hope.

When you created the heavens and the earth, you gave a variety of languages, different colors; but you also gave mankind one mind seeking truth and one heart seeking understanding.

Therefore we pray for understanding among the peoples of your world in their variety of tongues, in their differences of color, in their various national loyalties, and in their differing witnesses to you.

We pray that justice and freedom among the nations may establish that order which reflects your unity and the truth that you are.

O God of our fathers, of Abraham, Isaac, and Jacob, who have generation after generation raised up kings and prophets of the nations for your purposes of righteousness and peace, you undergird both statesmen who live in time and prophets who live in eternity as well as time.

So now we pray for all statesmen who represent their nation in the high councils of the nations,

—that they may be both statesmen whose task is to bring stability to the structures of society and also prophets whose vision judges every structure

—that they negotiate as statesmen to assure

permanence, and as prophets may never reduce justice simply to the pragmatic.

Keep them, we pray you, grounded in the affairs of men but always negotiating with you.

Help them as statesmen to adjust to the conflicting claims of people, and as prophets to adjust their will to your will.

May they bear the conflicting loyalties of their vocation with courage, perseverance, patience, and hope, confident that in your good time you will—through their faithfulness and our support—make these times better times; through him who is our present hope and eternal, Jesus Christ our Lord.

AMEN

For Peace

Almighty God, we pray for our troubled world and for peace among the nations. We recognize in our best moments that you are the creator of all mankind and not just *our* kind. Though we are tempted to believe that we have a special place in your kingdom, we realize that you have made of the same blood all your children and that you wish all members of your family well, that they may live in peace, harmony, and goodwill.

So strengthen the leaders of the nations who take counsel together to stay together in patience, to persevere in the search for peace, to listen to one another, and to be firm in their resolve to usher in a new day of freedom from fear, of justice for the oppressed, and of hope for all men. Give them a right judgment in all things that make for peace.

And that we may pray not only with our lips but with our lives, make us instruments of your peace. Where there is hostility, let us show love. Where there is hurt, let us heal. Where there is division, let us reconcile. Where there is doubt, let us bring confidence. Where there is sadness, let us be joyful. In all life may we be pleasant to one another—and toward you be full of joy, so that as we go about our days we may pray and sing of how good you are.

Keep in your safekeeping all those whom we love who are absent from us; to those who travel by land, by water, or by air give good judgment and a journey's end in safety. Especially do we pray for travelers through space that, speeding through the heavens, they may always come to a good landing on earth.

In all our comings and goings may we be with you and in you, who are yourself the source, the end, and the way of all journeys to our eternal destiny.   AMEN

After Watergate

Take from us, O God, all moral cowardice, every inclination to get along by going along. Confirm in us your spirit of integrity, that when we know what is right we may do it. Give us confidence that truth will prevail, so we may be loyal to truth and thus to you who art the Truth.

Grant that what we ask others to do, we may do ourselves, so that righteousness and peace may dwell in our land and the joy of the Lord be our strength under God.

AMEN

A Citizen's Prayer

Let us pay our taxes . . . obey the laws of the land . . . tell the truth . . . obey God rather than man if they are in conflict . . . be fearful only of not being true to our true selves . . . honor God, through Christ our Lord.

AMEN

PRAYERS FOR THE CHURCH YEAR

Advent

"The Light shines in the darkness, and the darkness never blows it out."

Lord Jesus,
 You are the Light of the World.
 Open our hearts, dark as they are, to let the
 Light in. Search us, even into the darkest
 recesses. Then come, live there full of grace
 and truth all the days of our lives—until you
 come again.

AMEN

Christmas

"Glory to God in the highest, and on earth peace, goodwill toward men."

Almighty God our heavenly Father, who have given us your Son to be our brother and our friend and by whose spirit we have now come together to sing the songs of Christmas:

We thank you for the vision of the shepherds at Bethlehem and for every vision of ourselves that you have given us. We pray that the vision they saw then and the vision we see now may be joined by your Son in making us more like him and our world more like his kingdom.

As gifts come to us, may we give to others. As peace is in our homes, may it come to the nations. As joy is in our hearts, may we rejoice in and work for the well-being of those who have no earthly cause for joy.

May we help one another bring to focus our common vision of a new day where brotherhood shall prevail, fears and poverty be no more, and where all your children may live in the spirit of your Son born this night into the human family and now born again in our hearts, to bring joy to all men, in every city and over the face of the earth.   AMEN

Epiphany

O come now, let us adore him
    as we bring him our most precious gifts—
    ourselves—
    in worship worthy of him.

AMEN

Ash Wednesday

For quiet on a quiet Ash Wednesday—
    our thanks.

For all our failures and sins—
    our confession.

For Lent—
    our anticipation.

For the people around us—
    our willing them well.

For our work—
    our dedication.

For colleagues—
    our thanks.

For our families—
    our gratitude.

For you—
    our honor.

So may this day begin a journey
    closer to you,
        with you,
            for you,
                in you,
                    Lord Jesus.

AMEN

Lent

Almighty God, we come into your presence to become truly present to ourselves and to you—at least as truly present as our consciences permit us.

So in the light of our consciences we examine ourselves. Since "in eternity conscience is the only voice that is heard" (Søren Kierkegaard) we ask for your spirit to help us look at ourselves in the light of your eternity. Your spirit searches all things, so help us now search ourselves.

It is not for your sake that we do this, but for ours. You already know all about us. We cannot tell you anything you do not already know about our sins—our broken promises and unfaithfulness, our pretense, pride, and double-mindedness, our wavering, faltering, drifting, our desire to be thought well of, rather than to do good or to be good.

You know these sins—the barriers between us and you. Help us to see them clearly as we name them and confess them to you . . . silently . . .

And now because the Eternal Word which prompts us to speak from our conscience is the Word spoken in Jesus Christ we thank you for absolving us, forgiving us, freeing us from those sins, for putting them away, removing them, so there are no longer any barriers between you and us. You make us once again pure in heart.

Help us now as we go through Lent to retain this purity by willing one thing only: to be responsible in all that we do, or say, or think, to you alone. When we are responsible to you, we are most responsible to ourselves,

149

and wholly free because we are in your service.

So, may the sins that we confess as the barriers between us become the bridge to a new life, lived wholly in you in the power of him who brings us to you, Jesus Christ our Lord.

AMEN

Good Friday

O Lord Jesus,
    We remember now on the eve of your betrayal, crucifixion, and subsequent redemption of the world by your obedience to your Father in remaining steadfast in your love of him and your fellowmen, that
        when Peter said he was ready to go with you to prison and to death you told him he would deny that he ever knew you.
    We come together in this place of remembrance and of prayer to tell you that in our best moments we want to be your disciples, and that this is now one of those moments.
    We would like to be as resolute as you were when you set your face toward Jerusalem,
        yet we know that most of our resolutions are like Peter's—faithful when all goes well, unfaithful when the going is difficult.
    This irresolution we now confess. We cannot justify ourselves any more than Peter could. We can only weep as he did.
    So, we pray that as you look now upon us as you looked upon Peter, you will take us up in your forgiving spirit and give us the courage to once again begin our discipleship. We know that if we are to be true disciples, we can do so only with your help.
    So help us.
    We take comfort in the knowledge that after you had remained faithful to your cross, you kept your trust in Peter and told him to feed your sheep.
    By that faithfulness of yours, help us to remain faithful to our crosses. Where we have much to bear, do you come to our aid to trust us and to strengthen us.

For we know we are never asked to bear more than we can bear.

So we give to you every burden—which we now name . . . of responsibilities . . . of people we are for . . . of decisions we must make . . . of circumstances we cannot control . . . of our lives, that we may live with hope, with confidence, and with joy. Give us your hope—your confidence—your joy.

And so shall we be transformed into faithful disciples—willing, eager, to follow you through life and death into the joy of everlasting life with you.

AMEN

Easter

"He is risen. The Lord is risen indeed!"

Our Father, yours is the kingdom of heaven and of earth, of everything that is and shall ever be. And your Son is our king. We pray that we may be loyal to him by what we do and who we are, so that all men may know that he is their king as well.

Our Father, yours is the power, so may we bear with everything in love in obedience to the laws of love and justice which prevail in your kingdom.

Yours is the glory. Therefore in all that we do and in all that we endure, in everything that we create, in everything that we affirm, may we give you the glory, for the glory is yours.

"He is risen. The Lord is risen indeed!"

So be it.

Yes.

AMEN

(Søren Kierkegaard, adapted)

153

Pentecost

The wind blows, God, just like your spirit.

It comes and goes any way you want it to because it is yours. You alone control it, direct it, make it strong sometimes, weak, or let it expire. It is your breath, and nobody owns it except you.

We can receive it. Wait for it. Be patient, expectant, hopeful. Be prepared for it.

We do this together; one mind, one spirit, one body, members of each other, concerned for one another, supporting one another. Waiting.

When the wind comes, it may come howling. Your spirit may howl, shaking, turbulent, as tongues of fire purifying, refining, burning up our dross, the tawdriness of our lives. Like a purifying fire, howling you may come. We wait.

Or gently the wind sometimes comes. So gently we can barely sense it stirring. We can't quite figure its direction. But we see a leaf quiver or a branch bend. Then we know it's here . . . blowing . . . gently.

So your spirit sometimes comes imperceptibly. Now we see it, now we don't. It comes, goes, returns . . . silently, gently. Suddenly we know life is all right, it goes on, we mustn't be afraid, nothing can hurt us, terrify us, destroy us.

Your spirit is very gentle, very powerful. You are very gentle, very powerful. *You* have come. So we wait.

You breathe. It is your breath. You breathe through us. We take a deep breath, inhale, exhale.

We are being breathed through—
through life and death
into eternity. By you.

We wait.   AMEN

154

Ascension Day

Ascended Lord Jesus, you are the leader who guides us on earth, and brings us to heaven.

Once you lived a human life, subject to the limitations of time; now you are the same yesterday, today, and forever.

Once you were limited to one particular place; now you are present whenever men turn to you.

Once only those who met you face-to-face knew you, and not all recognized you for who you were; now all men whose hearts are lifted in prayer to the unseen God know you dwelling in their hearts, and with you ascend to the heavens above, for your love knows no limits set by time or space, creed or race, sex or sin.

So, Jesus ascended,
Lord of life,
Above the heavens
Reigning,
Quietly, hiddenly
Praying in us,
We praise you.

AMEN